Whales, Dolphins, and More Marine Mammals

by **Sarah Gustafson** • with **Sarah Wilson** Consultant

SCHOLASTIC INC.

New York Toronto London Auckland Sydney Mexico City New Delhi Hong Kong Buenos Aires

Sarah Gustafson
WRITER

Sarah Gustafson writes about science from her home in the mountains of New Mexico. Although she's a land mammal, she loves swimming, body-surfing, and doing the dolphin kick.

Sarah Wilson
CONSULTANT

Sarah Wilson is a southern California native and now lives in the Florida Keys. She works with the dolphins and is the Assistant Director of Education at the Dolphin Research Center.

ISBN: 0-439-71189-4

Copyright © 2005 by Scholastic Inc.

Illustrators: Shawn Gould, Yancey C. Labat, Ed Shems, Zeke Smith

Photos:

Front cover: Marty Snyderman/Visuals Unlimited. Back cover: Flip Nicklin/Minden Pictures, photo obtained under NMFS permit #987. Title page: Brandon Cole/Visuals Unlimited.

Page 2 (shells): Photodisc Green/Getty Images. Page 7: (shark) James D. Watt/SeaPics.com; (whale) Doug Perrine/HWRF/SeaPics.com, taken under NMFS permit #587; (baleen) Michael S. Nolan/SeaPics.com. Page 8: (left) Alexis Rosenfeld/Photo Researchers; (middle) Dale Rice, National Marine Mammal Laboratory, NMFS, NOAA; (right) OAR/National Undersea Research Program (NURP); National Marine Mammal Lab. Pages 8–9: Doug Perrine/SeaPics.com. Page 9: (top) Phillip Colla/SeaPics.com; (bottom) Doug Perrine/SeaPics.com. Page 11: (whale) Mark Jones/SeaPics.com; (blubber) Tony Martin/Oxford Scientific. Page 13: Howard Hall/SeaPics.com. Page 18: (top) Phillip Colla/SeaPics.com; (middle) Mark Conlin/SeaPics.com. Page 19: (top) Jonathan Bird/SeaPics.com; (middle) Goran Ehlme/SeaPics.com; (bottom) John K.B. Ford/Ursus/SeaPics.com. Page 20: (top) Michael S. Nolan/SeaPics.com; (middle) James D. Watt/SeaPics.com; (bottom) Marilyn & Maris Kazmers/SeaPics.com. Pages 20: (top) Ingrid Visser/SeaPics.com; (bottom) Whale Watch Azores/SeaPics.com. Page 22: (left) Dave Fleetham/Pacific Stock; (right) Florian Graner/SeaPics.com. Page 23: Doug Perrine/SeaPics.com. Page 24: (top) Doug Perrine/SeaPics.com; (bottom) Hiroya Minakuchi/SeaPics.com. Page 25: Sarasota Dolphin Research Center. Page 29: Doug Perrine/SeaPics.com. Page 31: Joseph R. Olson/Cetacean Research Technology. Page 34: Marine Physical Lab at Scripps Institution of Oceanography. Page 35: (top) Stephen Frink/CORBIS; (bottom) Floris Leeuwenberg/The Cover Story/CORBIS. Page 37: (A) Amos Nachoum/SeaPics.com; (B) Gregory Ochocki/SeaPics.com; (C) Jeff Pantukhoff/SeaPics.com; (D and E) Doug Perrine/SeaPics.com. Page 38: Captain Budd Christman, NOAA Corps. Page 39 (seal) Bryan & Cherry Alexander/SeaPics.com; (sea lion) Phillip Colla/SeaPics.com. Page 41: Phillip Colla/SeaPics.com. Page 42: (top) Roy Tanami/Ursus/SeaPics.com; (middle) John Beatty/Photo Researchers; (bottom) Dan Guravich/Corbis. Page 43: (top) Doc White/SeaPics.com; (bottom) Kevin Schafer/SeaPics.com. Page 44: (manatees) Doug Perrine/SeaPics.com; (dugong) David B. Fleetham/SeaPics.com. Page 45: (top) Sam Javanrouh/wvs.topleftpixel.com; (middle) Kike Calvo/V & W/SeaPics.com; (bottom) Fritz Poelking/V & W/SeaPics.com. Page 46: (top) James D. Watt/SeaPics.com; (middle) Shedd Aquar/Lines Jr./SeaPics.com; (bottom) Steven Kazlowski/SeaPics.com. Page 48: Brandon Cole/Visuals Unlimited.

Whale and dolphin sounds provided by the Marine Physical Lab at Scripps Institution of Oceanography.

12 11 10 9 8 7 6 5 4 3 2 1   5 6 7 8 9 10/0

Printed in the U.S.A.

First Scholastic printing, May 2005

The publisher has made every effort to ensure that the activities in this book are safe when done as instructed. Adults should provide guidance and supervision whenever the activity requires.

Table of Contents

pages 16 and 32

page 30

Meet the Marine

Believe it or not, ocean explorer, you have a lot in common with whales, dolphins, seals, and walruses—not to mention sea otters and polar bears! What could you possibly have in common with all these different creatures? Well, for starters, you're all *mammals*. But unlike you, of course, these other mammals spend most of their lives in the water.

In this book, you'll find out what makes these water-loving mammals so well suited to living the marine life. Dive right in to discover the answers to questions like:

- What's the difference between a whale and a shark?

- How do marine mammals stay warm in cold water?

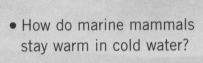

- What do whale songs sound like?

- Why are orcas called "killer whales"?

- How do dolphins see in the dark?

Which one am I again?

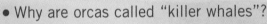

- What's the difference between a seal and a sea lion?

- How do sea lion mothers find their babies on a crowded beach?

- Which marine mammals use tools to eat their food?

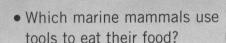

- What dangers do marine mammals face?

Mammals

What Is a Mammal, Anyway?

What makes a mammal a *mammal*, and not a fish or a frog or a lobster? All mammals—including you, ocean explorer—have five things in common:

1. We're Warm-Blooded

Even though some marine mammals live in freezing-cold water, they can make their own heat by converting their food to energy. This means they can keep their body temperatures pretty constant. The bodies of cold-blooded animals like fish, on the other hand, are about the same temperature as the water around them.

2. We Breathe Air

Ahhh...

Just like you, a whale has to hold its breath every time it dives underwater. Every mammal that swims has to come up for air. Other aquatic animals, such as fish and clams, get the oxygen they need by breathing water through their gills.

3. We Have Hair

Whales don't have heads of hair like you, but they do have whiskers when they're born! They lose their hair as they grow up. Other marine mammals, like otters and polar bears, have hair all their lives.

4. We Give Birth to Live Young

Unlike animals that lay eggs, a typical mammal carries her babies inside her body, attached by an umbilical cord, until they're ready to be born. That means dolphins have belly buttons!

5. We Nurse Our Young

Got milk? Whales do! Marine mammal milk contains lots of fat, which helps babies grow quickly. During the six or seven months a young blue whale drinks its mother's milk, it can gain 200 pounds (90 kg) a day—that's more than 8 pounds (3.5 kg) an hour!

So, now that you're up to speed on what it means to be a mammal, turn the page to plunge into the world of whales!

What's In Your Undersea Kit?

Whales and dolphins make noise underwater to communicate, to find their way around, and to locate prey. What do they sound like? And what's it like to listen in on the underwater world, anyway? Your Undersea Kit will help you find out!

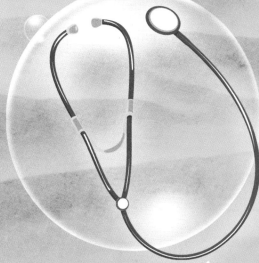

Underwater Listener
With this special microphone, you'll be able to hear noises underwater. Plunge to page 30 to soak up a whole new world of sound!

CD of Whale and Dolphin Sounds
Spin this disk to hear whales sing and dolphins squeak. Pages 16 and 32 will get you in the groove!

The Undersea University Website

Want more fun with marine mammals? Surf over to the Undersea University website (**www.scholastic.com/undersea**), where a new undersea challenge awaits! You'll find this month's password on the right.

WEB-SURFING PASSWORD

WHALEWATCH

PART I: Whales

Whales and dolphins belong to a group of marine mammals called *cetaceans* (sih-TAY-shens), which comes from a Greek word that means "sea monster." These mammals spend their entire lives in water. Most live in the ocean, but a few hang out in rivers or lakes. Some are so big, they would collapse under their own weight on land (without water supporting them from all sides)!

Shark or Whale?

At first glance, it's easy to confuse the two. After all, they have similar body shapes, with fins that stick up out of the water when they swim near the surface. Plus, they both can grow to be pretty big! But as you just learned, whales are mammals, while sharks are—you guessed it!—fish.

shark — breathes through gills

tail fin points up and down

The easiest way to tell a whale from a shark is to look at its tail. Sharks' tails point up and down, and they move their tails from side to side to swim. Whales and dolphins have flat tails that they move up and down to swim.

whale — breathes air through blowhole

tail fin is flat

Open Wide!

There are two types of whales: Some catch their food with *teeth*; others use plates of *baleen*.

The enormous "great" whales—such as the blue, gray, and humpback whales—all have baleen plates that hang like frayed curtains from the whale's upper jaw. Baleen whales filter water or mud to trap tiny sea creatures.

baleen hanging from upper jaw

Toothed whales, like the sperm whale, use their teeth to catch and hold fish and squid, then swallow their prey whole. Every year, a whale's tooth grows a new ring, just like a tree. Scientists can count the rings to figure out the whale's age!

What's Where on Whales?

If you had to do all your daily activities underwater, what would you wear? Fins on your feet for a stronger kick? Paddles on your hands to help you steer? How about a smooth, snug swimsuit so you slip through the water? Maybe even a snorkel tube so you could breathe without lifting your head?

A whale's body comes with all these features and more! You'll see a few on the whale on the right.

Dorsal Fin

Most whales have a top fin, or dorsal fin. Unlike the tail and flippers, the dorsal fin doesn't move. This fin keeps the whale from wobbling from side to side as it swims.

Powerful Tail

Made of bones and strong muscles, a whale's tail propels it through the water. The tip of the tail splits into two wing-like fins known as "flukes."

Tales of Whale Tails

Some whale species, like the humpback whale, have colored patterns on their tail flukes. Each humpback has a different pattern, just as each person has unique fingerprints. Scientists take photos of whale flukes year after year to study where particular whales go and how they behave. You can see just three examples of humpback tail flukes below.

Streamlined Body Shape and Smooth Skin

Picture a football. To help it fly through the air, it has rounded sides, and it's bigger in the middle than at each end. A whale has a similar shape. This streamlined shape and the whale's sleek skin help it glide through the water without wasting energy.

cloud of mist

Blowholes

What if your nostrils were on the top of your head, rather than on the tip of your nose? You'd barely need to poke your head above water to breathe! Well, that's where a whale's nostrils, or blowholes, are. When the whale comes to the surface for air, it blows out, sending a cloud of mist high into the sky. Then the whale takes a deep breath in through its blowholes before diving back underwater. Because it doesn't need to lift or turn its head like you would, a whale can breathe without slowing down.

Dwarf minke (MINK-ee) whales, like this one, are smaller than the more common minke whales. Dwarf minke whales often approach boats and swimmers along the Great Barrier Reef near Australia.

Flippers

Whales steer, balance, and brake using their paddle-shaped front limbs. Inside each flipper are bones similar to those in your arm and hand.

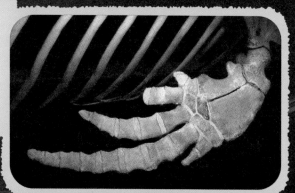

Staying Warm Underwater

When you're cold, ocean explorer, you might put on a sweater or turn up the heat. But whales have what they need to stay warm built into their bodies! This means whales and other marine mammals can spend most of their lives in super-cold conditions. How do they survive such low temperatures? Try on some blubber and some fur and find out!

What You Need

- Three large plastic bags with zip closures
- 2 cups of cooking shortening
- Bucket of ice water
- Thick sock

Your crew

- A friend

What You Do

Part 1: Try On a Blubber Glove

1. Put two cups of shortening in a plastic bag with a zip closure, leaving a space about the size of your hand in the middle of the glob.

2. Place an empty bag on each hand and have your friend zip them closed around your wrists.

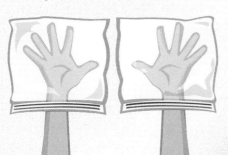

3. Put one hand into the bag of shortening and have your friend zip it closed around your arm. Then have your friend squeeze the shortening around until your hand is completely covered. The shortening represents the thick layer of fat on whales and other marine mammals.

4. Plunge both hands into a bucket of ice water. Does the shortening keep your hand warm?

Part 2: Warm and Fuzzy

1. After your hands have warmed up, put one bare hand inside a thick sock. This represents the thick fur that sea otters are covered in.

2. Leaving your other hand bare, place them both into the ice water. Leave them there until the sock is all wet. Which hand gets cold first? What happens when the sock gets completely wet?

Whales' blubber keeps them so warm that they can live in ice-filled waters.

Sea the Point?

In Part 1, you probably discovered that shortening kept your hand much warmer than a plain plastic bag did. This is because shortening is made of fat, which forms an insulating layer that keeps your body heat inside.

Fat insulates marine mammals in the same way. Most have thick layers of fat, called *blubber*, just under their skin, which helps them stay warm in very cold water. Like a life jacket, blubber also helps these animals float. The blubber layer of some whales is several feet thick!

In Part 2, the sock probably kept your hand from getting too cold—until the sock got wet. The same thing happens with fur, which is what sea otters rely on for warmth. (You'll find out more about sea otters on page 46.) When fur is dry, it holds air, providing a thick layer of insulation. But when cold water replaces the air, the fur loses its ability to trap heat. That's why sea otters spend lots of time rubbing their fur—they're adding tiny air bubbles to their fur for better insulation!

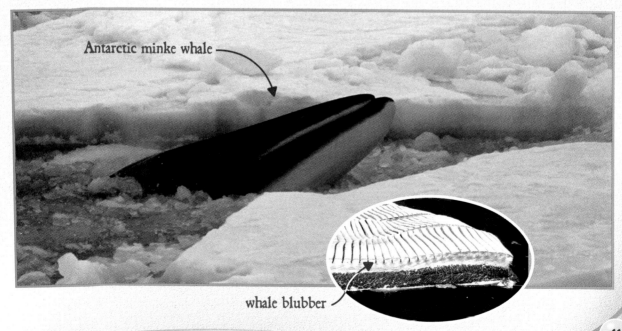

Antarctic minke whale

whale blubber

A Whale
of an Appetite

Big animals have big appetites! Read on to learn where and how three giant whales get their grub.

A Mouthful of Mud

Imagine if all your food was mixed into mud pies, and the only way to get to the good stuff was to take a big bite and spit out the mud. That's how a **gray whale** eats! First, it dives to the ocean floor. Opening its enormous mouth, it scoops up a mouthful of mud. Then it uses its tongue to push the water and mud out through its baleen (the comb-like plates that hang from its upper jaw). Thousands of small, shrimp-like animals that live in the mud get stuck behind the whale's baleen. All the whale has to do now is lick the inside of its baleen and swallow its meal!

Humpback Hunting Habits

Did you know that **humpback whales** blow bubbles to catch their food? Working together, they swim around a school of fish, blowing small bubbles as they go. This creates a bubble net around the fish. Scientists don't understand exactly why, but fish won't swim through this net of bubbles! The whales then swim up inside the bubble net with their mouths open wide, devouring the fish stuck inside. You can try out bubble nets for yourself in the Sea Quest on page 14!

And the Champion Diver Is...

How long can you hold your breath, ocean explorer? Thirty seconds? A minute? The world record for a human is just over eight minutes. But that's not much compared to **sperm whales**, which can hold their breath for almost two hours! This means they can dive deeper than any other marine mammal, reaching 2 miles (3 km) or more below the surface. What's the point of diving so deep? Because that's where sperm whales' prey lives! These whales eat lots of squid, including the giant squid, which is as long as a sperm whale itself!

It's So Great to Migrate

Every year, the largest whales travel thousands of miles. They spend the summers feeding in icy waters near the North and South Poles. Then they migrate to warm water to have their babies. What does it take to travel that far? Read on!

gray whale

Stocking Up for the Journey

Gray and humpback whales can eat a ton or more of food every day, which means they can store plenty of energy. When it's time to migrate, they can travel up to 100 miles (160 km) a day without eating!

The gray whale migrates farther than any other mammal, swimming from the Arctic seas to Mexico and back—up to 14,000 miles (22,500 km) round trip! During their migrations, the whales spend almost three months swimming without stopping to eat, living off the fat stored in their blubber.

Measure Your Migration

How far do you "migrate" in a day? Just follow these three steps to find out.

1. Locate a map of your neighborhood so you can measure distances. If needed, ask a parent to show you how to read your car's odometer.

2. Keep track of every place you go in one day. How many miles do you

MIGRATION
To School: 4 miles
To Soccer Practice: 2 miles
Home: 6 miles

Total: 12 miles

travel to school? To your best friend's house? How about to soccer practice or music lessons?

3. Add up all these measurements. How far did you "migrate"? How does your journey compare to that of a gray whale, which can swim up to 100 miles (160 km) a day—without a car to carry it around?

Filter for Your Food

Many whales get their food by filter feeding—straining ocean water through the baleen plates in their mouths and eating the krill and other small creatures that are left behind. What's it like to eat like a whale? Tuck in your napkin and break out the baleen, because it's time to find out!

What You Need

- Chocolate sprinkles
- Small bowl of water
- 6 tablespoons of dried parsley or another herb
- Large bowl of water
- Plastic comb that fits inside the large bowl
- Measuring cup
- Three paper towels
- Four straws

Your Crew

- A friend (optional)

What You Do

Part 1: Snaring Sprinkles!

Not in the mood for krill? That's okay—in this part of the Sea Quest, you'll get a feel for filtering chocolate sprinkles instead!

1. Scatter some chocolate sprinkles into a small bowl of water.

2. Standing over a sink, pour some of the water into your mouth, but don't swallow. Let the water flow out of your mouth and into the sink, and hold onto those sprinkles!

3. Continue filter feeding until you've trapped all the sprinkles. How many mouthfuls of water did you have to take in?

Part 2: Skim, Gulp, or Bubble?

Just as some people pick up pizza with their hands while others use a knife and fork, baleen whales have a variety of methods to get their munchies into their mouths. Here's your chance to test a few, using a comb as baleen!

1. Sprinkle 2 tablespoons of dried parsley into a bowl of water. This represents krill in the ocean.

2. For your first test feeding, skim the top of the water with a comb, catching as much prey as you can. Wipe the parsley onto a paper towel.

3. For your second test, add more parsley to your "ocean" and scoop up some water with a measuring cup. Pour it out through the comb so the prey gets stuck between the teeth while the water flows through. Wipe this parsley onto another paper towel.

4. For your final test, add a bit more parsley. Using two straws, blow gently into the water to push the parsley toward the center of the bowl. If you have a friend handy, have your friend blow through two more straws to help herd your parsley prey. When you have as much as possible in one place, scoop it up with your cup and filter it through your comb as you did in step 3. Wipe the parsley onto the third paper towel.

5. Compare your paper towels. Which has the most parsley? Which feeding method was easiest?

Sea the Point?

In Part 1, did you press your top and bottom teeth together to keep the sprinkles in your mouth while letting the water flow out? If so, your teeth were acting like a whale's baleen, filtering the food from the water. You probably went through a lot of water for a small bite of sprinkles. Can you imagine how much water a whale must filter to fill its belly? That's why a **humpback whale** has a stretchy throat, so it can fill its mouth with thousands of gallons of water at once!

What did you think of the various feeding styles in Part 2? When you skimmed the top of the water with your comb, you fed like a **bowhead whale**, which swims along the water's surface with its mouth open wide, skimming off snacks as it goes.

With your measuring cup, you imitated the enormous throat of a **blue whale**, which takes in huge gulps of water, then pushes the water back out through its baleen. The krill get left behind on its baleen just like the parsley stuck to your comb. This is also the method you used to eat your chocolate sprinkles!

Finally, you created a bubble net (swim back to page 12 to learn more). You probably found it best to blow toward the center of the bowl from different directions. To catch schools of small fish, **humpback whales** work together to surround their prey with bubbles!

Which method got you the most parsley? You may have found one method was easier than another. Whales feel the same way! Like all animals, each type of whale has a feeding style that suits it best.

Songs of the Sea

Suppose you lived underwater and wanted to get in touch with some friends far away. You could write letters, but the paper would probably fall apart before it got there. You could give them a call, but telephones don't work well when wet. Or you could yell very loudly—and they just might hear you!

Because sound travels both faster and farther through water than through air, it's an excellent way to communicate in the sea, even across great distances. Most baleen whales have deep voices that travel very far, letting them stay in touch with one another and attract mates across the ocean.

You can listen to all sorts of whale noises on the CD of Whale and Dolphin Sounds that came in your Undersea Kit!

Music Across the Miles

Humpback whales are famous for their sounds. Males make a series of different noises that they string together to form a long, complex pattern called a *song*. They can sing the same song for hours and hours, and these songs can travel up to 6 miles (10 km) away! Humpbacks sing the most around breeding season. Scientists think their songs might be a way for them to attract females and to tell other males to stay out of their way.

humpback whale

The blue whale call is the loudest in the sea. It can be so low-pitched that the human ear can't hear it. But other whales can, even from *thousands* of miles away!

blue whale

How Does Sound Get Around?

Sounds travel in waves that spread out from the source, like ripples in a pond where a pebble has been dropped. Unlike light, sound can travel through solid things (like rocks), as well as through gases (like air) and liquids (like water).

Different sound waves have different amounts of distance between the ripples, or *cycles*. High-pitched sounds, like the whistles of the dolphin on track 2 of your CD of Whale and Dolphin Sounds, are made by short waves that have lots of cycles per second. Low-pitched sounds, like the moans of the baleen whale on track 1 of your CD, are made by long waves with fewer cycles.

Lower sounds travel farther than high-pitched ones, which is why baleen whales' low noises are great for long-distance communication! Why do low sounds travel farther? Since their waves are very long, they cover much more distance per cycle than the short waves of high-pitched sounds. This means they can travel a longer way before running out of energy.

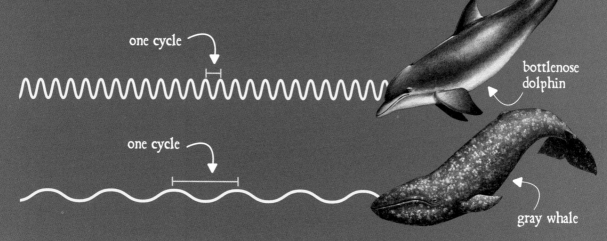

one cycle

one cycle

bottlenose dolphin

gray whale

Make Some Noise

A whale doesn't have vocal cords like humans do. It makes noise by squeezing air through spaces in its head called *sacs*. Want to give it a try?

mini Quest

1. Play the CD of Whale and Dolphin Sounds from your Undersea Kit. Listen carefully, noticing all the different sounds you hear.

2. Blow up a balloon. As you let the air out, stretch the open end of the balloon in various ways to make as many different noises as you can. How do your "songs" compare to those of a humpback whale (track 1)? A dolphin (track 2)?

3. Now you've seen how a balloon compares with the noises of whales. How does your *voice* compare? A sperm whale can "vocalize," or make noise, for almost two hours on a single breath. See how long you can vocalize before coming up for air! Inhale deeply and start talking—and see how long you last.

You're probably wondering which whales make the other sounds on your CD. To find out, try the Sea Quest on pages 32–34!

A Trail of Whales

The Great Big Blue

A blue whale
seen from above

Just how big is a **blue whale**, the largest animal that's ever lived on our planet? It's so huge that it's hard to even imagine its size without comparing it to other things! Here are a few examples:

- The blue whale can grow up to 110 feet (34 m) long—about as long as three school buses parked end-to-end.

- It can weigh up to 200 tons—almost twice as much as the biggest dinosaur.

- An elephant could fit on a blue whale's tongue.

- The whale's heart alone weighs as much as a small car and pumps 10 tons of blood through its huge body. You could crawl inside the whale's main blood vessel!

Here you can see how enormous a blue whale skeleton is compared to a person!

Long Live the Bowhead!

This big whale lives in the frigid waters of the far north, rarely far from ice. In fact, it can break through sheets of ice a foot thick when it needs to breathe!

If it escapes hunters, a **bowhead whale** can live to a pretty ripe old age. One bowhead found in Alaska was more than a hundred years old—and scientists in California believe they may even be able to live twice that long.

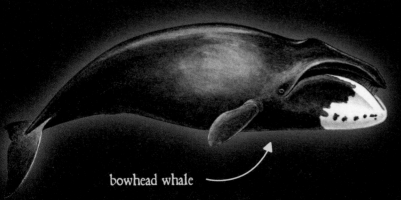

bowhead whale

The Chatty Beluga

If you're ever sailing the waters near the North Pole and you hear mooing, clicking, squeaking, and whistling, you're probably listening to a **beluga whale**. Nicknamed *sea canaries*, belugas are toothed whales that make a huge variety of sounds.

Because they can change the shape of their lips, belugas often seem to smile or frown. Belugas are also the only whales that can turn their heads! That's because the bones in their necks aren't fused together the way they are in other whales.

A baby beluga is born gray, and it gradually turns lighter as it grows. By the time it's nine years old, the beluga has turned pure white—the better to blend in with icebergs! Every summer, it sheds its skin, sometimes rubbing itself on rocks on the ocean floor.

Because beluga whales lack dorsal fins, they can swim easily under sheets of ice.

A group of narwhals swimming near the surface

Unicorn of the Sea

The **narwhal** is a toothed whale that has just two teeth—but in male narwhals, one of these teeth grows right through its upper lip to form a spear-like tusk up to 9 feet (2.7 m) long. Traders in the Middle Ages tried to keep the existence of the narwhal a secret so they could sell its long tooth as a unicorn horn!

A narwhal poking its head above water

Pardon My Breach

humpback whale

Do you like diving into the water? Well, whales and dolphins seem to enjoy diving into the *air*. Many whales *breach*, leaping way out of the water and landing with an impressive SPLASH! Humpback, gray, and sperm whales breach more often than others, but even a 150-ton blue whale can leap into the air!

Why do whales breach? No one knows for sure, but here are some ideas:

sperm whale

- **They're trying to get the attention of other whales.** Breaching makes a lot of noise, and sound travels far underwater. Whales may be saying, "Hear my splash—here I am!"

- **They're showing off!** Males throughout the animal kingdom display their strength to attract mates. Male whales may breach to prove how big and powerful they are.

- **They're getting rid of parasites.** Small creatures such as barnacles and lice may live on a whale's skin. Sounds itchy, huh? Maybe whales breach to shake off some of these creatures.

gray whale

- **They're playing.** After all, isn't that why *you* dive?

Save the Whales!

If you were a whale, what animal would you fear most? Sharks? Killer whales? Polar bears? All of these creatures prey on whales, but in fact, humans are whales' worst enemies by far.

For centuries, people have hunted whales for their meat as well as for their blubber, which has been used in products from machine oil to suntan lotion—even in crayons! Pollution is another major threat to whales. Toxins that collect in a whale's body can weaken its ability to fight off disease. As a result of things people do, many whales are in danger of going extinct.

Stranded!

Whales are also in danger of *stranding*. This happens when whales swim right up onto beaches—and get stuck there. Scientists don't know why this happens. Perhaps the whales were escaping from predators, needed a resting spot, or simply got lost.

Rescue teams shade stranded whales to protect them from sunburn, and they keep the whales' skin wet until they can be moved back into the water.

Once they're stranded, some whales fall over onto their sides on the beach. When the tide comes in, water covers their blowholes before they can right themselves, and they drown. Fortunately, people have formed rescue teams around the country to help stranded animals recover and return to the sea.

A biologist guides a whale back out to sea.

Dolphins and Porpoises

What's the Difference Between a Dolphin and a Whale?

If you think this is a trick question, ocean explorer, you're right—dolphins *are* whales!

Remember back on page 7 when you learned about the two main types of whales: baleen and toothed? Dolphins and porpoises belong to the group with teeth. In general, they stay near the water's surface, swim very fast, and are really smart. Here's how to tell dolphins and porpoises apart:

Porpoises have a flat face with no beak. They spend most of their time in shallow water near coastlines.

Dolphins have a long, pointed nose called a *beak*. They live in both deep and shallow water.

Both have an oil-filled organ called a *melon* in their foreheads. This melon is no relation to a cantaloupe! Find out what this organ does on page 26.

INFO BUBBLE
When the bottlenose dolphin sleeps, only half of its brain rests at a time! The other half stays awake to watch for predators, swim, and come up for air. After a couple of hours, the dolphin switches sides!

Welcome to My Pod

Like peas, dolphins live in groups called *pods*. Read on to find out about the three main types of dolphin pods!

Maternity Pods

Have you ever heard of a "playgroup," where groups of moms and children get together? Well, *maternity pods* are the playgroups of the dolphin world. They're made up of female whales and their young, which are called *calves*.

Dolphin calves stay in the maternity pod for three to six years. Even after their calves leave, older mother dolphins will remain in the maternity pod, helping young mothers learn how to be good moms.

Juvenile Pods

When young dolphins are old enough to leave their mothers, but not ready to have babies of their own, they form *juvenile pods*. Males hang out with other males, and females with females. The males and females interact with one another, but they won't be ready to mate for a few more years.

While in a juvenile pod, young dolphins practice their social and hunting skills until the females return to a maternity pod (as mothers, this time) and the males form bachelor pods.

Bachelor Pods

When male dolphins outgrow juvenile pods, they team up with one or two other mature males to form a *bachelor pod*. The pod travels, hunts, and looks for females together. The guys become very close—it's like being best friends forever!

Dolphins tend to have many friends. They greet each other by *raking*, or rubbing their teeth on each other's skin. That sounds a lot more painful than shaking hands, doesn't it? Dolphins do get bite marks and scratches, which heal in time.

rake marks

Going on a Fish Hunt

If dolphins got report cards, they might include comments like "Works well with others." Members of a pod work together to take care of sick or injured friends and to catch fish and squid. Several pods may travel and hunt together in large herds made up of hundreds of dolphins. By working cooperatively, these herds can even attack sharks!

Below you can find out more about the crafty hunting tactics dolphins use to catch a meal.

- **Beaching Breakfast**
Along muddy shorelines, dolphins chase fish all the way out of the water and onto the beach. Then the dolphins swim onto the shore, grab the fish, and slide on the slippery mud back into the water.

- **Mud Ring Munchies**
In shallow water, dolphins stir up mud from the seafloor by swimming in circles near the bottom. Fish won't swim through this wall of mud, but they will jump over it. Now all the dolphins have to do is poke their beaks above the surface and catch the fish flying through the air.

- **Have a Ball!**
In deep water, dolphins swim in tight circles around a school of fish, herding their prey into a tight ball known as a "baitball." Then the dolphins take turns diving through the center of this feast, gobbling as they go. At the top of this page, you can see the bottom of a huge baitball!

Dr. Randall Wells

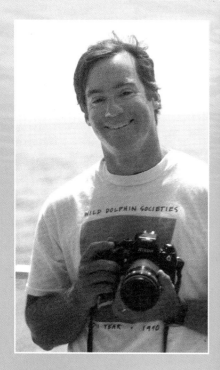

Dr. Randall Wells began working with bottlenose dolphins in high school, as a volunteer at Mote Marine Laboratory in Sarasota, Florida. Thirty-five years later, he's still studying the same group of dolphins, researching how they live and how to protect them. Dr. Wells oversees the Sarasota Dolphin Research Program, operated by the Chicago Zoological Society and based at Mote Marine Lab.

Question: What can you tell us about the dolphins you study in Sarasota Bay?

Answer: There are about 150 dolphins that use the bay on a regular basis. The community is like a small town, where you know almost everyone, and most of your family lives there generation after generation.

Q: How can you tell the dolphins apart?

A: We can identify dolphins based on their dorsal fin shape, especially nicks and notches along the back edge. We've put together a catalog of more than 2,500 dolphin dorsal fins from the central west coast of Florida (including the ones from Sarasota Bay).

Q: What's the hardest part of your job?

A: Emotionally, the hardest thing is when we recover a dead dolphin that we've known for a long time. It's like losing a member of the family. Even harder is learning that the dolphin died because of humans. So a large part of what we do involves educating people.

Q: What's it like to rescue a dolphin?

A: It's incredible. One dolphin we'd known since birth was dragging great big balls of fishing line, which was cutting through her tail flukes. We were able to use a boat hook to grab the line and cut most of it off. Then she swam next to our boat for more than half an hour and let us try to get the rest of the line off of her. It seemed clear the dolphin recognized we were trying to help her.

Q: If you have to bring a sick or injured dolphin to the hospital, how do you return it to its natural habitat?

A: If we recognize the dolphin from our catalog of dorsal fins, we can put it right back where it came from. Because these animals spend their entire lives in one location, their ability to survive depends on being in the area they're used to, with dolphins they know.

In 1990 we returned two captive bottlenose dolphins that had been out of the wild for two years. We released them where they came from and have kept an eye on them ever since. They fully readapted to life in the wild!

25

Seeing the Sea with Sound!

The ocean can be a dark and murky place sometimes, especially down deep, where sunlight doesn't reach. How do animals see where they're going? Dolphins and other toothed whales have a special sense called *echolocation*. As you might have guessed from the name, this sense uses *echoes* to *locate* things.

How Does Echolocation Work?

To create an echo, a dolphin uses its *melon* to send a sound wave that our ears perceive as a *click*. When the wave reaches an object—such as a tasty fish—it bounces off and echoes back to the dolphin. The sound then travels through a fat-filled bone in the dolphin's lower jaw to its inner ear, which sends a message to its brain. The whole process can take less than a second!

dolphin sends out sound waves

dolphin receives echo waves

Do You See What I Hear?

Using echolocation, dolphins can figure out the size and shape of an object, as well as how far away it is, how fast it's moving, and in what direction. They can even tell if a fish is dead or alive! A dolphin can also use the echoes it receives to create a map of its surroundings. When exploring an area, the dolphin sends out slow clicks. Once it's located something interesting, it clicks faster to get more precise information.

Biologists have discovered that dolphins can see an object with their eyes, then find the same object using only echolocation. You could say that echolocation allows dolphins to *see* with sound!

Can You See Me Now?

In the ocean, dolphins can detect objects from 300 feet (91 m) away—that's as far across as a football field! How well can you "get the picture" from *half* that distance?

1. Grab a friend, a measuring tape or yard stick, and a bag of small toys or stuffed animals of various sizes, shapes, and colors. Head to a large open area, like a playground or ball field.

2. Measure 15 feet (4.5 m) on the ground, and count how many steps you take to go that far.

3. Multiply your number of steps by 10 to find out how many steps you need to take in order to travel 150 feet (45 m). Starting next to your friend, walk 150 feet away.

4. Have your friend hold up the toys one by one. Can you recognize them?

5. If not, walk forward until you can identify the toys correctly.

How close did you have to get? Using echolocation, dolphins can recognize objects from twice as far away as you started out!

Turn It Down!

If you had to find your next meal just by listening for it, ocean explorer, could you do it? That's exactly how dolphins hunt, using echolocation (flip back a page if you missed this). Try this version of the game "Marco Polo" to find out how you'd do as a dolphin!

Sea Quest

What You Need

- Large room or open area outside
- Blindfold
- Radio or CD player

Your crew
- A few friends

What You Do

1. Choose your hunting grounds—you'll need an open area with at least several feet in all directions.

2. Choose one person to be the dolphin. Everyone else gets to be a fish.

3. Blindfold the dolphin. This person has to find the fish by calling out and listening for the echoes, just like dolphins do. Each time the dolphin calls out "dolphin," the fish must say "fish" in response.

4. The dolphin should keep calling out "dolphin" until he or she can tag all the fish. How long does it take?

4. Now turn on some music and try the game again. Does that make it harder for the dolphin?

Sea the Point?

In this Sea Quest, you located your friends dolphin-style—by listening for responses to your sounds. Of course, dolphins can hear their *own* sounds come back to them, whereas you had to have your friends help out to create an echo. But you should have gotten a pretty good idea what it's like to echolocate!

Was it harder to find the fish when you listened for them over the sound of music? Dolphins may have the same problem! Between sounds from boat engines, ships' sonar, machines digging for oil, and other human activities, people make a lot of noise in the ocean.

Some scientists think these unnatural sounds, called *noise pollution*, make it harder for dolphins to echolocate. Dolphins may have to find new ways to hunt for food to adapt to this challenge!

If You Need Me, Just Whistle!

So you've learned about the sounds dolphins make to see. How about the sounds they make to *speak*? Dolphins talk a lot, using mostly high-pitched whistles to communicate among themselves.

HI! MY NAME IS FLIPPER!

I'M MARINA!

Wet Your Whistle

Each dolphin seems to have what scientists call a *signature whistle*. Like a name tag or an ID card, this whistle identifies an individual dolphin. Just as your parents named *you*, a dolphin's mother teaches her calf its whistle. Remember how wobbly and unclear your letters looked when you first learned to write your name? It takes a dolphin several months to get the hang of making *its* signature whistle, too.

MAY I HEAR YOUR SIGNATURE WHISTLE PLEASE?

By whistling, dolphins let others in their pod know who's around and where they are. If a young calf becomes separated from its mother, they both whistle repeatedly until they find each other.

Are You Talking to Me?

In addition to whistling its own name, a dolphin can imitate the signature whistles of others. Why do they do this? Scientists aren't sure, but they think it may be to get a particular dolphin's attention—sort of like yelling, "Hey, Joe!"

Hey! That's MY whistle!

A Barking Dolphin?

Dolphins make other sounds as well, including chirps, pops, barks, and kitten-like mews. Biologists think these noises are ways of greeting each other, showing interest in each other, or showing that they're upset or angry. And when hunting, dolphins can produce loud, low-pitched sounds that seem to stun or even *kill* fish. Scientists don't fully understand how, but the burst of sound these dolphins create produces a strong wave that can seriously injure their prey.

Listen Up!

How can a scientist listen to whales and dolphins without diving underwater? And what if scientists want to *record* sounds to listen to later, or to analyze on a computer?

That's where *hydrophones* come in. Perfected during World War I so scientists could locate enemy submarines, hydrophones are basically microphones that work underwater.

With hydrophones, scientists can listen in on the undersea world, hearing all kinds of sounds—like whale and dolphin noises. In this Sea Quest, you'll use *your* underwater listener to listen in on your own watery world—your bathtub!

What You Need

- Blindfold
- Bathtub full of water
- Underwater listener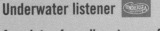
- A variety of small, waterproof objects from around the house, such as bouncy balls, paper clips, and small toys

Your Crew

- A friend

What You Do

Part 1: Direction Detection

How well can you tell where a sound is coming from? Does listening underwater make a difference?

1. Wearing a blindfold, sit in the middle of a quiet room.

2. Have your friend walk silently into a corner of the room and say "hello."

3. Without peeking, point to the place where you think your friend is standing. Are you right?

4. Now, head to the bathroom to find out how well you do underwater. Put your blindfold back on, place the hearing end of your underwater listener in the tub, and put the earpieces in your ears.

5. Have your friend tap on one side of the tub. Can you tell which direction the sound is coming from now?

Part 2: What's That Noise?

Now that you've got the hang of listening underwater, put your hearing to the test!

1. With your blindfold and underwater listener in place, have your friend drop small objects into the tub, one by one. Listen carefully to the sound each object makes as it lands on the bottom of the tub. Can you guess which is which?

2. Switch places and have your friend try.

3. Find out how noises on the surface of the ocean sound from underwater. Start with some rain! Have your friend turn on the faucet just enough to produce a slow, steady drip. How does the sound compare above and below the water? What about splashes—how do they sound?

Sea the Point?

In Part 1, did you have a hard time telling which direction sound came from underwater? If so, you're not alone! Scientists have the same problem. This is why they use several hydrophones placed in a row to pinpoint the source of whale songs and other sounds. Depending on where the song is coming from, its sound waves will arrive at each hydrophone at a different time, because each one is a different distance from the whale.

Did you know your brain uses the same type of system? When your friend called to you from across the room, the voice reached each of your ears at a slightly different time. Your brain used this info to figure out where the sound came from. If you had only one ear, it would have been harder to figure out where your friend was standing!

In Part 2, how well could you tell sounds apart underwater? On page 29, you learned that dolphins recognize each other by their *signature whistles*. The things you dropped into the tub each have a signature sound as well. In the next Sea Quest, you can listen to the sounds of some real dolphins and whales!

Here, researchers are using a hydrophone to listen to dolphin sounds. With a computer, they can see graphs of the sound while listening to it. In the next Sea Quest, you'll find out more about these graphs!

Name That Tune!

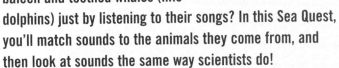

Now that you've heard the noises everyday objects make underwater, it's time to find out what marine mammals sound like! Can you tell the difference between baleen and toothed whales (like dolphins) just by listening to their songs? In this Sea Quest, you'll match sounds to the animals they come from, and then look at sounds the same way scientists do!

What You Need

- CD of Whale and Dolphin Sounds
- CD player
- Pencil and paper

What You Do

Part 1: Baleen or Teeth?

Back on page 7, you learned the difference between baleen and toothed whales. These two types of whales also *sound* different! Take a listen.

I. Listen to track 1, the song of a humpback whale. Like other baleen whales, humpbacks sing in low-pitched, mournful moans.

2. Listen to track 2, the song of a common dolphin. Like other toothed whales, dolphins make high-pitched whistles, squeaks, and clicks.

3. On your paper, write the numbers 1–15. Now listen to the rest of the songs on your CD. Based on what you just learned in steps 1 and 2, which sounds are baleen whales, and which are toothed whales? Write down your answer next to each number.

Part 2: Melody Match

Now, see if you can take a step further and identify specific animals! Read the descriptions below, then listen to tracks 3 through 7 again. Which whale sang which song? Write its name next to the matching track number on your paper.

Commerson's Dolphin

Can you hear this dolphin repeat the same set of rapid clicks several times? This is the sound of the dolphin using echolocation!

Gray Whale

This baleen whale creates a series of funky popping or drumming sounds in addition to burps and growls.

Sperm Whale

The sperm whale makes a series of fast clicks in rhythmic patterns. It sounds a little like horse hooves on pavement.

False Killer Whale

This whale is famous for its whistle-like call, which sounds almost like a bird's song.

Fin Whale

Instead of moaning like other baleen whales, this whale produces pulses of sound at a regular rate.

Part 3: Seeing Sound

Did you know that scientists can make pictures of sound? On the right, you'll find several *spectrograms*—graphs that show what sounds look like. Scientists use these graphs to see things they might not hear, such as small details or sounds that are too low or too high for the human ear to detect.

Take a close look at Spectrogram A on the right. You can see how many seconds the song lasts by looking at the numbers along the bottom. The numbers on the left tell you how high or low the sound is (called *pitch*, which you learned about on page 17). Each sound in the song shows up as a mark on the graph. The low-pitched sounds are low on the graph; the high-pitched sounds go up higher. And the brighter the mark, the louder the sound.

The sound in Spectrogram A looks like it begins with a low-pitched tone, then a high-pitched one, followed by another low-pitched note, and then two more that are high-pitched. And that's all in the first four seconds! Listen carefully to tracks 6 through 10 again. Do any fit this description?

Now that you know how spectrograms work, listen to tracks 6 through 10, then match each with its spectrogram!

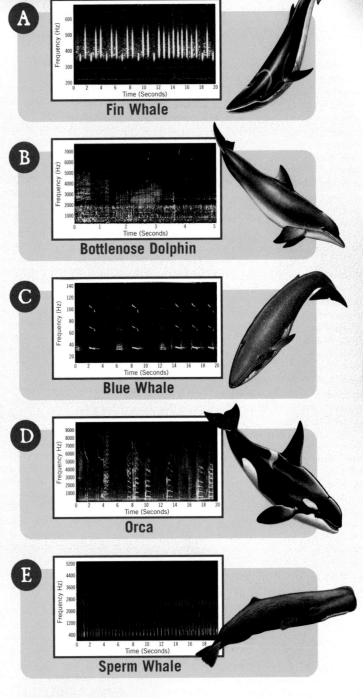

A Fin Whale

B Bottlenose Dolphin

C Blue Whale

D Orca

E Sperm Whale

How'd You Do?

Swim on over to page 48 to check your answers. Could you figure out which whales made which sounds? You're probably also wondering which whales made the sounds on tracks 11–15. You'll find that info on page 48, too.

Dolphins and YOU!

There's something very special about our relationship with dolphins. After all, they're among our closest relatives in the ocean. It's hard not to wonder what they're thinking, or what it's like to live in such a different world.

And maybe they wonder the same things about us! Dolphins seem very curious about humans. They often swim close to boats, sometimes leaping and flipping as they ride the waves the boat creates. Dolphins even catch waves with surfers and check out scuba divers underwater. They've also been known to help out when humans need them. How? Read on!

Go Fish!

Bottlenose dolphins near a village in Brazil have been working with humans to catch fish since 1847. When the dolphins line up near the shore, the fishermen know it's time to wade into the water with their nets. Then the dolphins swim toward the beach, herding fish as they go. They signal the men to cast their nets with a special dive. While the fishermen fill their nets, the dolphins fill their bellies with fish that try to swim back to sea.

Helping or Hurting?

Feeding wild dolphins may be fun for humans, but it's bad for the dolphins! It teaches them to beg from boats, which puts them in danger of being hit by fast-moving boat traffic.

Feeding also encourages dolphins to get food from people, rather than from the ocean—so they never learn to hunt!

Stay Safe!

In 2004, a group of swimmers near a New Zealand beach suddenly found seven bottlenose dolphins swimming in tight circles around them, herding them together. The dolphins circled around them for forty minutes, slapping the water with their tails. A lifeguard who came by on a rescue boat saw why: There was a great white shark in the water nearby! The dolphins stayed with the swimmers until they came safely to shore.

Name That Dolphin!

Grab your binoculars, ocean explorer—it's time to head out on a dolphin watch! You're about to meet five new dolphins. Based on the descriptions below, can you figure out which is which?

What You Do

Read the descriptions below, then match each dolphin on the right with its description. You can check your answers on page 48!

I. Thanks to movies and TV shows, this species often comes to mind when people hear the word "dolphin." Like many movie stars, the shape of its mouth seems to form a permanent smile! These dolphins will often chase each other, toss seaweed back and forth, and carry objects around. Why? Scientists think the dolphins may be practicing their hunting skills!

2. Also known as the *pink dolphin* because of the color of its skin, this dolphin lives in fresh water near a rain forest. During floods, the dolphin can swim right through the surrounding

What You Need
- Your dolphin-spotting smarts

forest! Because it lives in very muddy water, it relies almost entirely on echolocation to navigate and find its food—including the famous piranha.

3. This dolphin can leap 10 feet (3 m) high and turn around like a top while in mid-air! It can make up to four complete circles before splashing back into the water.

4. The unique hourglass pattern on this dolphin's side could be why artists have been painting portraits of it since the time of the ancient Greeks. Thousands of these dolphins travel together, sometimes all coming up for air at the same time—what a sight! They swim fast and leap high, often flipping in mid-air. They're also known for catching a ride on the waves that form in front of ships and large whales.

5. How did this dolphin get a nickname like *killer whale*? Long ago, sailors who saw them eating other whales began calling them whale killers. Eventually, the words got rearranged. Known as "wolves of the sea," some of these dolphins hunt in packs. By working together, they can kill animals much larger than themselves, including the gigantic blue whale! But don't worry—they don't attack people.

A Orca

B Amazon River Dolphin

C Common Dolphin

D Spinner Dolphin

E Bottlenose Dolphin

Seals, Walruses, and Manatees

Presenting...the Pinnipeds!

Now that you're an expert on whales and dolphins, it's time to meet some marine mammals who spend some of their lives on land. You'll travel to sandy beaches, rocky islands, and big chunks of floating ice, where you'll find all sorts of seals, sea lions, and walruses.

These animals make up the group called *pinnipeds* (PIN-uh-peds), which comes from Latin words meaning *fin foot* or *feather foot*. Pinnipeds spend most of their time in the water, where they use their four webbed flippers for swimming. But when it's time to mate, give birth, or molt (shed their fur), most come ashore, some for weeks at a time. Then their flippers become their feet!

What Else Do Pinnipeds Have in Common?

- Like cats and dogs, pinnipeds eat meat. Some like fish and squid, and others prefer clams or crabs. The bigger pinnipeds, like some sea lions and walruses, sometimes dine on seals. Leopard seals, the most fearsome predators in the Antarctic, will eat penguins and even the pups of other types of seals!

- To keep warm, pinnipeds have thick layers of blubber. They also have fur coats, which they shed each year. Without their fur, some seals don't have enough insulation to stay warm in the water. They have to wait onshore until their new coat grows in. Since they can't hunt while they're molting, they live off the fat in their blubber.

● Although pinnipeds don't have fingers, that doesn't mean they can't touch the world around them. They have very sensitive whiskers that send information to their brains about what things feel like. These whiskers help them find food in the water and friends on a crowded beach.

How to Tell SEALS from SEA LIONS

back flippers
behind body

ear holes

seal

furry and clawed
front flippers

ear flaps

long and
furless
front
flippers

sea lion

back flippers
under body

FEATURE	SEAL	SEA LION
Ears	• Small ear hole on each side of head	• Ear flaps around ear holes
Front Flippers	• Short and furry, with long claws	• Long, furless, and wing-like
Back Flippers	• Short and furry • Drags these behind its body, almost like a tail	• Long and furless • Can rotate these underneath its body, until they face forward, like feet
Moving on Land	• Pulls itself forward with front flippers and flops along the ground like a caterpillar	• Brings all four flippers under its body and walks like other four-legged animals • Can even climb tall rocks and stairs!
Sounds	• Burp sounds and quiet barks	• Loud barks and roars

Are You My Mother?

California sea lions like to hang out in *big* bunches. Hundreds may gather on the same beach to give birth in noisy groups known as *rookeries*. If you were a

mama sea lion in a crowded rookery, could you listen and sniff your way to your pup? Try this Sea Quest to find out how hard that might be!

What You Need

- Five film canisters (or any small container)
- Paper clips and marbles (or other small objects)
- Six cotton balls
- Cinnamon and garlic powder (or two other spices)
- Tape

Your Crew

- A friend

What You Do

1. Fill two film canisters with paper clips, and fill two more with marbles. The containers should be about a third full.

2. Sprinkle cinnamon on two cotton balls, then turn them upside down so you can't see the cinnamon. Tape one cotton ball to one container of paper clips, and tape the other to a container of marbles.

3. Sprinkle garlic powder on two more cotton balls. With the garlic powder side down, tape these cotton balls to the other two filled containers. You should now have four containers with a scent on top and an item inside: cinnamon paper clips, cinnamon marbles, garlic paper clips, and garlic marbles.

4. Step out of the room, and while you're gone, have your friend fill the fifth container with either paper clips or marbles and tape on a cotton ball with either cinnamon or garlic powder.

5. Come back into the room, and take the mystery container your friend has prepared for you. This is your imaginary sea lion pup! Gently shake it and sniff it to get used to its sound and smell. Remember them both, because you can't inspect your pup again!

6. Now take a break and have a chat with your friend (real sea lions would be off catching fish). After five or ten minutes, shake and sniff the four film canisters you filled in steps 1–3. One of these should have the same sound and smell as your "pup." Can you find it?

7. Was that too easy? To make it more challenging, get some more film canisters and try the activity with additional scents and sounds!

Sea the Point?

Could you remember the sound and smell of your "pup" well enough to find its match? If so, perhaps you should consider a career as a California sea lion!

Soon after a baby sea lion is born, the mother and pup talk to each other and sniff each other repeatedly until they form a lasting memory of what the other sounds and smells like. Scientists call this *imprinting*, and it's fairly common among mammals and birds.

The mother stays near her pup for a week or so, nursing and protecting it. But then she must leave her pup on the beach for several days at a time, while she swims out to sea to hunt for fish and squid. When the mom returns to the rookery, she barks and sniffs until she finds her pup among the many on the beach.

INFO BUBBLE

Although California sea lions have a powerful sense of smell on land, they can't smell well underwater!

A California sea lion rookery in Mexico

Seals with Appeal

Rudolph the Red-Nosed...Seal?

Imagine if you had a bright red balloon attached to your nose. When you blew out through one nostril, the balloon would inflate. Wouldn't that be a great way to get attention? That's how **hooded seals** do it! Males have what's called a *nasal sac* that they inflate to attract females and scare off other males during the breeding season.

What's Big, Gray, Has a Trunk...and Swims in the Ocean?

If you said "an **elephant seal**," then you get a *seal of approval*, ocean explorer! Elephant seals have a large nose that resembles an elephant's trunk. If a male seal (or *bull*) feels threatened, his trunk-like nose will inflate and he can use it to snort a loud challenge to other males. Elephant seals are also the largest pinnipeds in the world, even bigger than walruses!

The Hidden Harp Seal

If you were born on the ice, but grew up in the water, what would you wear to stay warm and to protect yourself from polar bears, killer whales, and sharks? You might want to check out **harp seal** coats. A harp seal pup is born covered in thick, white fur that helps it blend in with the snow-covered ice. Within a few weeks, it sheds its white coat and grows a spotted gray coat that provides camouflage in the water, where the growing seal spends most of its time hunting for fish and shrimp.

Year after year, the harp seal sheds its old coat and grows a new one, each with a slightly different pattern. After four or five years, the harp seal has silvery-gray fur with a black head. Many also sport a big, black U-shaped spot across their back that looks like—you guessed it—the musical instrument for which this seal is named.

harp seal pup

spot looks like a harp when seen from above

A Whale-Horse? Whoa!

What do you call an enormous red mammal with two long tusks and a bushy mustache, whose babies sometimes ride on its back? Early Dutch hunters called this creature a "whale-horse," a name that's evolved over the years into *walrus*.

Walruses have features in common with both seals and sea lions. Like seals, they lack ear flaps on the outside of their heads. Like sea lions, they can turn their hind flippers forward in order to walk on all fours. When a walrus is in a hurry, it can move on land as fast as a man can run!

Tusk, Tusk!

How 'bout those tusks? They're actually teeth that never stop growing! In the icy Arctic waters where walruses live, these teeth come in quite handy.

When a walrus wants to come ashore, it anchors its tusks in the ice to help pull its huge body out of the water. If it needs to create a breathing hole or rescue a calf that's stuck, it can use its tusks to break up the ice. After all that work, if it just wants to rest in the water, it can hook its tusks over the edge of the ice while it floats.

Males also use their tusks to fight over females and to fight for space in crowded areas. Sometimes they end up with cuts and scars on their necks and shoulders.

Ready, Set, Blow!

When it's lunchtime in the Arctic, a walrus heads for the bottom of the ocean. There it squirts powerful jets of water out of its mouth, spraying clams and other shellfish loose from the seafloor. But that's not all! The walrus can also use the vacuum power of its large cheeks to suck the clams right out of their shells. An adult walrus may eat as many as 6,000 clams a day!

INFO BUBBLE

In really cold water, a walrus's blood moves inward to keep from losing heat, making the animal's skin appear almost white!

Mermaid or Manatee?

manatee

Okay, ocean explorer, take a careful look at this picture of a manatee. Does it look like a mermaid to you? Apparently it did to early sailors who reported seeing graceful sea creatures with the body of a woman and the tail of a fish. Maybe they'd been out at sea just a little too long!

Siren Song

Manatees, along with their closest living relatives, the dugongs, belong to a group of animals called *sirenians* (sye-REE-nee-uns), from the Greek word

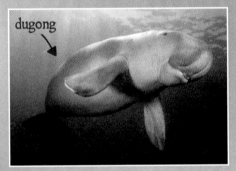
dugong

seiren (or siren). According to Greek legend, sirens were sea spirits who lived on a rocky island, singing magical songs that caused sailors to crash into the rocks and drown.

In the real world today, sirenians have much more to fear from humans than the other way around! Because they move slowly and live in shallow coastal waters, manatees and dugongs make easy prey for hunters. Many others are hit by boats. As a result, their populations have been decreasing. In the United States, the Marine Mammal Protection Act makes it illegal to hurt any type of marine mammal. In some parts of the world, however, manatee meat is available for sale.

What a Cow!

The only vegetarians among all marine mammals, manatees and dugongs spend their days grazing on sea grass and weeds. They can eat as much as 200 pounds (90 kg) of food every day!

Along the southeast coast of the United States and in the Gulf of Mexico, you may be lucky enough to see the West Indian manatee, which can grow almost as big as a minivan! Here you can see a mother manatee, called a cow, with her calf.

PART 4: Polar Bears and Sea Otters

Have you thought about toes lately? If not, it's time to start. Check out the feet on your nearest dog or cat. See how each of their toes is separate from the others? Scientists put animals with toes like those in a special group called *fissipeds* (FISS-uh-peds), which means *split foot*. The final marine mammals you'll meet, polar bears and sea otters, also belong to the fissiped club.

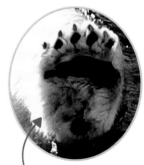

the polar bear's foot

The Bear Necessities

Although polar bears live on the ice and snow surrounding the North Pole, they're considered marine mammals because they get their food from the water and are very strong swimmers. With extra-large feet that are slightly webbed, they can swim more than 60 miles (100 km) a day. The bottoms of their feet are covered with small bumps and dense fur that keep them from slipping on the ice.

A polar bear can swim for hours at a time.

Positively Polar

How does the bear stay warm when the temperature drops far below freezing? In addition to a thick layer of blubber, a polar bear has black skin and clear, hollow hair, both of which soak up heat from the sun. The bear's fur looks white only because it reflects the color of ice and snow! Oils in the thick coat repel water and keep the bear dry.

Polar bears are the largest four-footed carnivores on Earth, but they start out blind, toothless, and not much bigger than a chipmunk. Newborn cubs will stay in their dens for several months, and then stick close to their mothers for two to three years.

You Otter Use Some Tools!

Would you believe that the marine mammal most closely related to a skunk eats at a table, with utensils? That's right, ocean explorer—the sea otter is among

the few animals that use tools and furniture. The otter hunts for food underwater, diving to collect sea urchins, clams, crabs, and other hard-shelled creatures with its front paws. Then the otter comes to the surface, where it floats on its back. Using its belly as a table, it places a rock on its chest and smashes its prey against the rock to break open the shell.

But that's not all! Sea otters have a pouch of loose skin under each front leg. They stash their rocks and food in these pockets while they dive, leaving their paws free for hunting.

Furry Facts

Remember back on page 10 when you learned about keeping warm underwater? Unlike other marine mammals, sea otters lack blubber. Instead, they have the thickest fur of any animal—up to 1,000,000 hairs per square inch. You probably don't have more than 100,000 hairs on your whole head! In order to stay dry, a sea otter spends hours each day rolling in the water and rubbing itself to keep its fur clean and fluffed full of air. Because of this layer of air and natural oils from its skin, the otter never really gets wet! But if its fur gets very dirty, it can die from the cold in less than a day.

A mother otter can use her body as a cradle, carrying her pup on her belly until it's old enough to swim and dive on its own. When she needs to hunt, she wraps her pup in strands of seaweed to protect it and keep it from drifting away.

Eat Like an Otter

Could you eat like an otter? It might be harder than you think. Since otters don't have a layer of blubber under their skin like other marine mammals, they have to eat a lot of food to keep warm in cold water. That's why otters make sure to get a lot of it! Try this Sea Quest to see how your appetite compares.

What You Need

- Paper and pencil
- Your food's packaging
- Small kitchen or postal scale (optional)
- Calculator

What You Do

1. Before you eat breakfast, make a list of everything on your plate. Find out how much each item weighs in grams, either by reading the "Nutrition Facts" on the back of the food's packaging, putting the food on a small scale (don't forget to subtract the weight of the plate!), or asking an adult to help you guess.

2. Keep track of everything you eat throughout the day. Make sure to include your snacks!

3. At the end of the day, add up your grams. To find out how many pounds of food you ate, divide the total by 454. How does the weight of one day's food compare to how much you weigh? How do you think it compares with what an otter would eat in a day?

Sea the Point?

As an animal digests food, that food turns into energy, some of which heats the animal's body. So, eating is a great way for an otter to stay warm! A typical otter grows to be about 4 feet (1.2 m) long and weighs between 54 to 70 pounds (25 to 32 kg)—probably about the same size as you. But an otter digests its food a lot faster than you do in order to produce enough heat! To keep up, it needs to eat about 15 pounds (6.8 kg) of food a day. That's about one-fourth its weight! You probably found that your total was much lower than that.

So, ocean explorer, how much would you have to eat to match an otter? Imagine chowing down on a cheeseburger, small fries, and a small strawberry shake. Are you full? If you weigh 65 pounds, you'll need to eat more than 16 meals that size—all in one day!

Whale Meet Again!

So, ocean explorer, now you've got the inside scoop on the wonders of whales, dolphins, and other marine mammals. You've tested out blubber, used your nose and ears like a sea lion, and even tried eating like a whale and an otter! *Plus* you've tuned in to all kinds of underwater sounds—everything from humpback whale songs to splashes in your bathtub!

That's all for this Undersea University book—but don't hang up your dive gear yet, because many more ocean adventures await you at UU!

THE ANSWER KEY

▶ Pages 32–34: **Name That Tune!**

Parts 1 and 2:
1) Humpback whale (baleen)
2) Common dolphin (toothed)
3) False killer whale (toothed)
4) Gray whale (baleen)
5) Commerson's dolphin (toothed)
6) Fin whale (baleen)
7) Sperm whale (toothed)
8) Blue whale (baleen)
9) Bottlenose dolphin (toothed)
10) Orca (toothed)
11) Beluga whale (toothed)
12) Risso's dolphin (toothed)
13) Northern right whale (baleen)
14) Baird's beaked whale (toothed)
15) Long-finned pilot whale (toothed)

Part 3:
A) Fin whale (track 6)
B) Bottlenose dolphin (track 9)
C) Blue whale (track 8)
D) Orca (track 10)
E) Sperm whale (track 7)

▶ Pages 36–37:
Name That Dolphin!

1) E 2) B 3) D
4) C 5) A